BY
JOANNA BRUNDLE

PHOTO CREDITS

VOLCANOES
AND EARTHQUAKES

CONTENTS

Words that look like **this** can be found in the Glossary on page 31.

WHAT ARE EARTHQUAKES?

Imagine! The ground is rumbling under your feet. Suddenly, it starts to jerk violently from side to side or up and down. Buildings are shaking and starting to crumble. The road beside you cracks and splits. It's an earthquake!

Earthquakes are very common, occurring somewhere in the world about twice every minute. Every year around one hundred of these cause damage, but most last less than a minute.

A catastrophic earthquake hit Kathmandu, Nepal on 26th April 2015. It killed nearly 9,000 people.

The point where an earthquake happens, under the surface of the Earth, is called the focus. The epicentre is the place on the surface of the Earth that is directly above the focus. It is usually the place that shakes the most. Energy blasts out from the focus in the form of shock waves, just like ripples when you throw a stone into a puddle. These shock waves are called seismic waves and they can travel for thousands of kilometres. Seismic waves that travel along the Earth's surface are called surface waves.

Earthquakes can cause other natural disasters, like landslides, avalanches and flooding. It is these natural events that can kill many people.

Smaller tremors often happen before and after the main shock of an earthquake. Those that happen before the main shock are called foreshocks and those that happen after it are called aftershocks.

The deadliest earthquake that ever occurred happened in Shaanxi, China in 1556. Around 830,000 people were killed.

WHAT ARE VOLCANOES?

Deep within the Earth lies super-hot molten rock called magma. Magma is full of gas bubbles and is less dense than the rock above it. Being lighter, it tries to rise above the solid rock and to escape by breaking through the Earth's surface. Volcanoes are places where it erupts.

Magma from the chamber pushes up the conduit and out of the vent. At the surface, it is called lava. As the hot lava flows downhill, it cools and forms a cone.

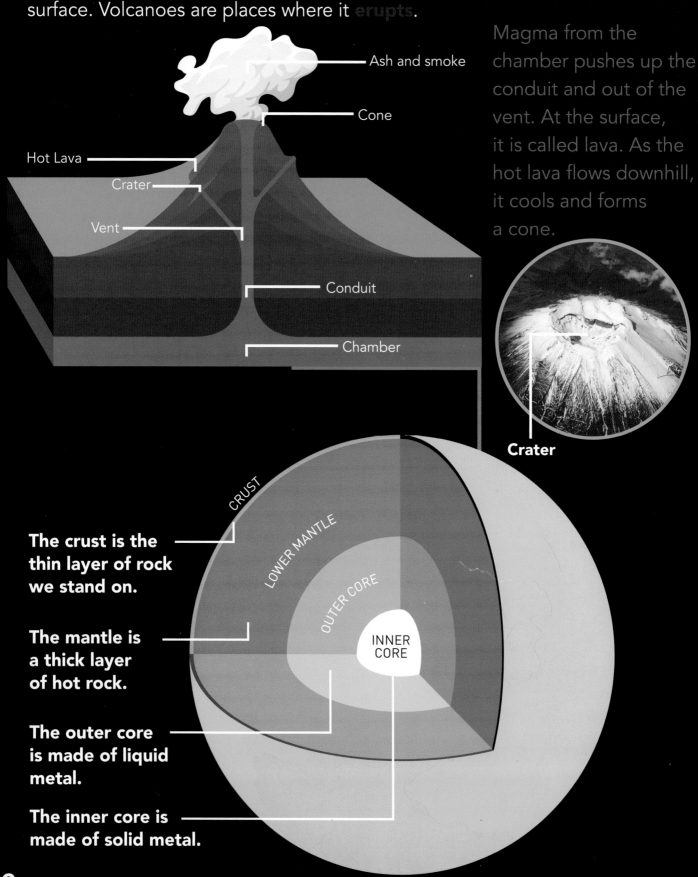

Ash and smoke

Cone

Hot Lava

Crater

Vent

Conduit

Chamber

Crater

CRUST

LOWER MANTLE

OUTER CORE

INNER CORE

The crust is the thin layer of rock we stand on.

The mantle is a thick layer of hot rock.

The outer core is made of liquid metal.

The inner core is made of solid metal.

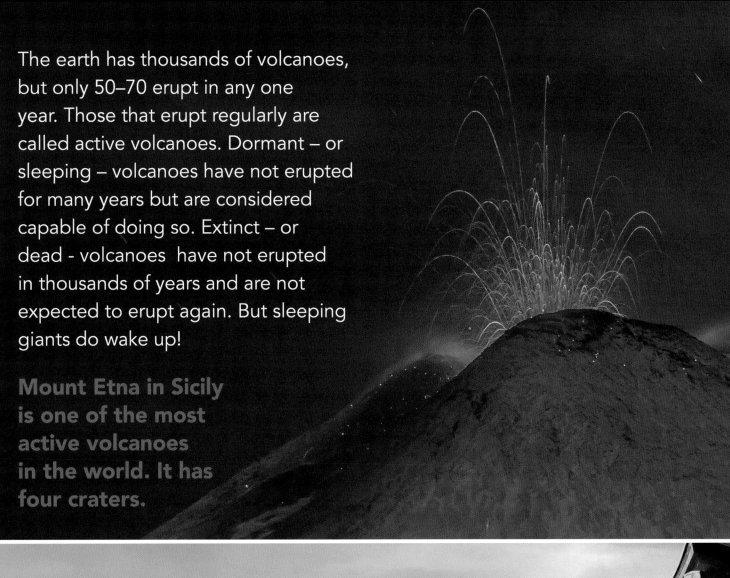

The earth has thousands of volcanoes, but only 50–70 erupt in any one year. Those that erupt regularly are called active volcanoes. Dormant – or sleeping – volcanoes have not erupted for many years but are considered capable of doing so. Extinct – or dead - volcanoes have not erupted in thousands of years and are not expected to erupt again. But sleeping giants do wake up!

Mount Etna in Sicily is one of the most active volcanoes in the world. It has four craters.

Mount Fuji in Japan last erupted in 1708 and is considered dormant.

WHAT CAUSES EARTHQUAKES AND VOLCANOES?

The outer layer of the Earth – the crust – is like a giant jigsaw puzzle made up of huge slabs of rock. It feels solid under our feet doesn't it? In fact, the giant slabs, called tectonic plates, are constantly moving as they ride on top of the layer of molten rock underneath. They move very slowly, at about the same rate as your fingernails grow. That's up to seven centimetres a year.

If the Earth was the size of an apple, the crust would be thinner than the apple's skin.

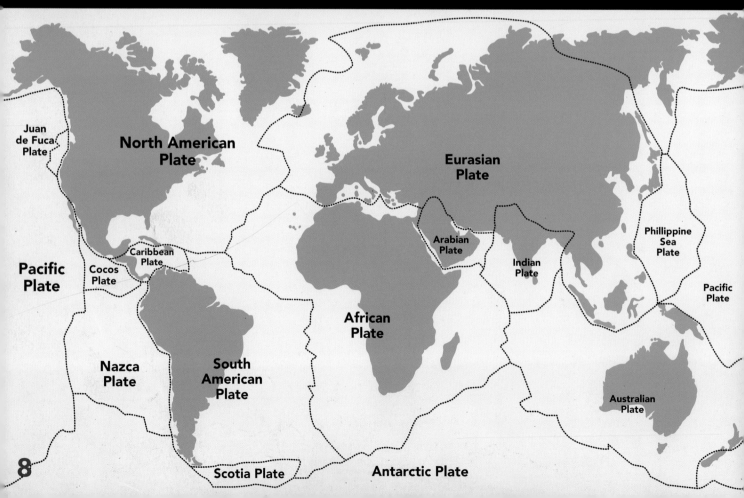

Juan de Fuca Plate

North American Plate

Eurasian Plate

Arabian Plate

Phillippine Sea Plate

Indian Plate

Caribbean Plate

Pacific Plate

Cocos Plate

Pacific Plate

African Plate

Nazca Plate

South American Plate

Australian Plate

Scotia Plate

Antarctic Plate

As they move, tectonic plates come together in different ways. They may meet head on, grind sideways against one another, pull apart or slip underneath each other. The moving plates create huge amounts of pressure, which can cause cracks on the Earth's surface called faults or fault lines.

The San Andreas Fault in California, USA is about 30 million years old and is about 1,300 kilometres long. You can see it from space and it marks where the North American Plate meets the Pacific Plate.

Fault line in Pingvellir National Park, Iceland

9

Plate boundaries are areas where plates come together. Most volcanoes are formed along plate boundaries. Some occur where magma rises up to fill a gap caused by plates pulling apart. Sometimes, one plate sinking and melting beneath another causes an eruption. But not all volcanoes form along plate boundaries. Hot spots are places where super-hot magma forces its way through the middle of a tectonic plate.

Volcanic eruptions at a hot spot in the Pacific Plate formed the islands of Hawaii. These islands form a chain because, while the plate kept moving, the place where the super-hot magma spewed out was not moving.

All around the edge of the Pacific Ocean are plate boundaries where the Pacific Plate meets other plates. There are so many volcanoes in this region that it is known as the "Ring of Fire".

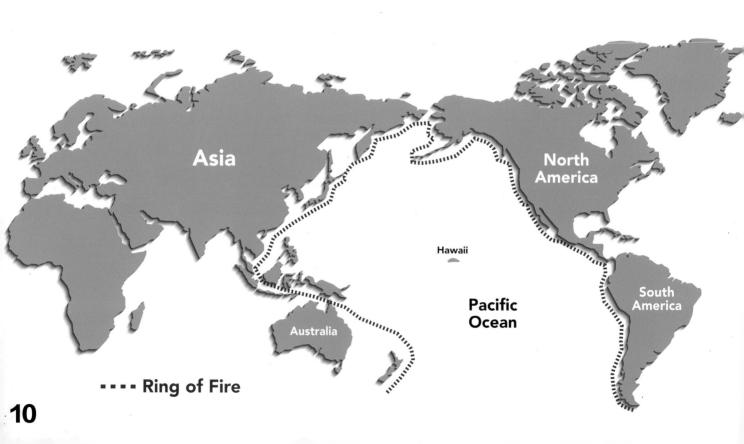

Asia

North America

Hawaii

Pacific Ocean

South America

Australia

- - - - Ring of Fire

Scientists know that most earthquakes occur along fault lines. The force applied by tectonic plates that are moving causes huge amounts of rock along a fault line to slip suddenly and violently. When this happens, the energy is released as shock waves that make the ground shake. Think of pushing your hands together to snap a stick. Pressure builds, the stick breaks and you can feel shock waves up your arm.

Haiti is a very poor country that suffered a serious earthquake in 2010. Poorly constructed buildings collapsed and around 230,000 people died. Fewer people die in earthquakes in richer countries, where safer but more expensive building materials are used.

THREE KINDS OF FAULT

01 > **NORMAL FAULT**
Top layer of crust moves down.

REVERSE FAULT
Plates squeeze together.
Top layer of crust moves up. **02**

03 > **STRIKE-SLIP FAULT**
Blocks of rock grind past one another.

DIFFERENT KINDS OF VOLCANO

Mauna Loa, a shield volcano in Hawaii, is the world's largest active volcano.

The shape of a volcano depends on the type of volcanic material that it spews out. Magma can be thin and runny or thick and sticky, depending on the temperature of the molten rock as well as the gases and **minerals** inside it. Shield volcanoes form when fast-flowing runny lava spreads out over a wide area, forming a gently sloping mountain.

Cinder cone volcanoes form when lumps of sticky magma erupt violently into the air. The lumps cool into cinders and pile up to form small, steep volcanoes.

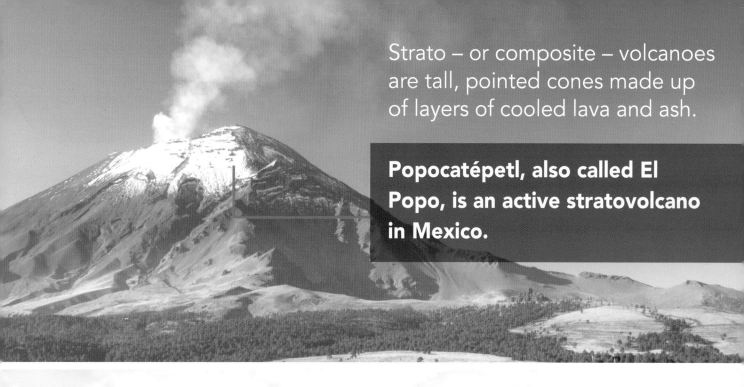

Strato – or composite – volcanoes are tall, pointed cones made up of layers of cooled lava and ash.

Popocatépetl, also called El Popo, is an active stratovolcano in Mexico.

Sometimes a volcano erupts so violently that the magma chamber is emptied. The volcano collapses in on itself, leaving a hollow, ring-shaped crater called a caldera. A crater lake is a caldera that has filled with water.

The Quilotoa caldera in the Andes mountain range, South America.

Many volcanoes erupt under the sea. The water causes the lava to cool quickly and the volcano keeps growing until it reaches the surface, forming a volcanic island.

The Galápagos Islands were formed from undersea volcanoes, which are called seamounts.

13

VOLCANIC MATERIAL

Pahoehoe Lava

Black smokers are dark, smoky jets of water that form around underwater volcanoes. Small particles build up to form tall, black chimneys.

Some kinds of lava can have unusual names. As it cools, thin, runny pahoehoe (say pa-hoy-hoy) lava forms a wrinkled skin that looks like coils of rope. Thick, sticky aa (say ah-ah) lava is spiky and jagged. When underwater volcanoes erupt, the cooling action of the water forms smooth, rounded pillow lava.

Pele's hair lava is made up of thin strands of volcanic glass. It is named after Pele, the Hawaiian goddess of volcanoes.

Pele's Hair Lava

A house destroyed by ash on the slopes of Mount Merapi, the most active volcano in Java, Indonesia.

A pyroclastic (say pie-row-klas-tic) flow is a boiling-hot mass of volcanic ash, rock and gas that races down the mountain at speeds of up to 200 kilometres per hour.

Volcanoes do not erupt mud, but a mudslide is one of the greatest dangers of an eruption. Mudslides - or lahars - form when water, either from heavy rain or snow melted by a pyroclastic flow, mixes with volcanic ash and dust.

Sometimes, as molten lava cools to form rock, the minerals inside it form precious crystals, such as diamonds.

MEASURING EARTHQUAKES AND VOLCANOES

Seismologists are scientists who study earthquakes. They use equipment called seismographs and information from satellites to see where the tectonic plates are moving and where an earthquake may happen.

Spikes in the line record strong tremors.

Scientists use the Richter Scale and the Moment Magnitude Scale to measure the strength of earthquakes. The higher the number is, the stronger the earthquake.

A seven or more on the Richter Scale is a major earthquake. The Mercalli Scale describes what people experience during an earthquake, for example a four means parked cars rock from side to side.

Scientists who study volcanoes are called volcanologists. As well as working in laboratories, they visit volcano sites, sometimes while the volcano is actually erupting. It's dangerous work! Wearing goggles, masks and special suits like this to protect them from the heat, they collect gas and lava samples.

A **supervolcano is a massive eruption. Yellowstone National Park, USA is the site of a supervolcano that last erupted 640,000 years ago. It spewed out enough ash and gas to block out the Sun and plunge the world into darkness. Scientists think it could erupt again - but not in our lifetime!**

Volcanologists use the Volcanic Explosivity Index, or VEI, to measure volcanoes. A supervolcano scores eight.

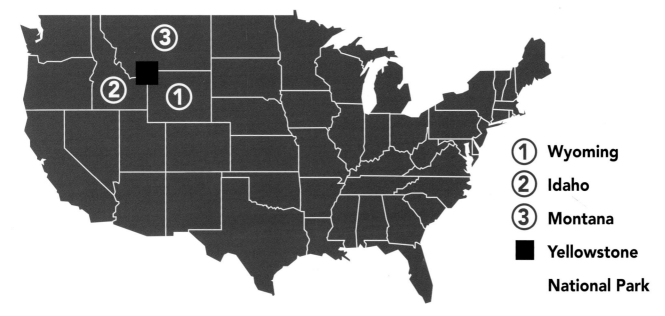

1. Wyoming
2. Idaho
3. Montana
■ Yellowstone
National Park

SURVIVING EARTHQUAKES AND VOLCANOES

Buildings in earthquake zones can be built to withstand the shaking of an earthquake. Layers of rubber and steel between the buildings and their foundations absorb shock waves, just like your trainers when you run. Steel beams strengthen walls and reduce the amount of shaking. Upper floors that can sway a little help to stop buildings collapsing by changing some of the earthquake's energy into movement.

Following an earthquake, rescue teams are often helped by search dogs who are trained to smell people buried under the wreckage.

Children practise this drill in earthquake regions.

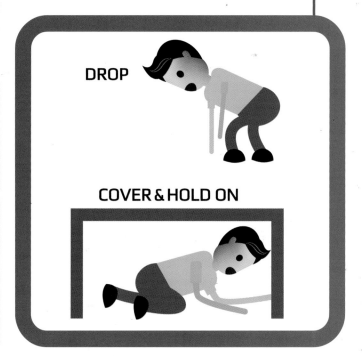

DROP

COVER & HOLD ON

The rubber pads in the base of the Transamerica Pyramid in San Francisco helped it to survive a large earthquake in 1989.

HOW TO SURVIVE A VOLCANO

01 **Evacuate** your area as quickly as possible if you are told to do so. Don't stop to collect your belongings.

02 Stay **upwind** of a volcano to protect yourself from ash and poisonous gases.

03 Wear a mask or goggles and cover your skin.

04 Stay away from any channels, such as river valleys, where lava might collect.

05 Volcanic lakes may contain enough acid to burn your skin, so don't swim in them!

An acidic crater lake in The Philippines

THE SAN FRANCISCO EARTHQUAKE 1906

San Francisco, USA stands on two fault lines - the San Andreas Fault and the Hayward Fault. In 1906 it was a busy trading city, second only to New York. But on the 18th of April, a huge earthquake, measuring 8.2 on the Richter Scale, struck. The main shock lasted over a minute. Fires started as broken electrical wires sparked and soon the city was engulfed in flames. Around 2,000 people died and 300,000 people lost their homes.

San Francisco on fire after the earthquake.

City Hall was destroyed.

THE INDIAN OCEAN TSUNAMI 2004

A tsunami (say soo–nar–mee) is a series of waves caused by volcanic eruptions or earthquakes under the sea. As the fast-moving waves approach land, they slow down and gain height, causing disastrous damage as they crash onto the shore. The Indian Ocean tsunami was caused by a violent earthquake that happened out at sea. The waves caused by the earthquake were 15 metres high when they hit the land and travelled at speeds of up to 800 kilometres per hour.

COUNTRIES WORST AFFECTED BY THE TSUNAMI

(1) Indonesia   (7) Myanmar

(2) Malaysia   (8) Kenya

(3) Thailand   (9) Tanzania

(4) Sri Lanka   (10) Somalia

(5) India   (11) Seychelles

(6) Bangladesh   (12) Maldives

● Earthquake epicentre

Tsunami damage in Aceh, Indonesia

Indian Ocean

The tsunami made 2 million people homeless.

CATASTROPHE IN JAPAN 2011

Japan sits on a fault line where the Pacific and Eurasian tectonic plates meet. It is well prepared for earthquakes, but the force of the earthquake which struck on 11 March 2011 caught everyone by surprise. Measuring a massive 9.0 on the Richter Scale, it happened 130 kilometres off the coast, but was strong enough to rock buildings in Tokyo, 370 kilometres away.

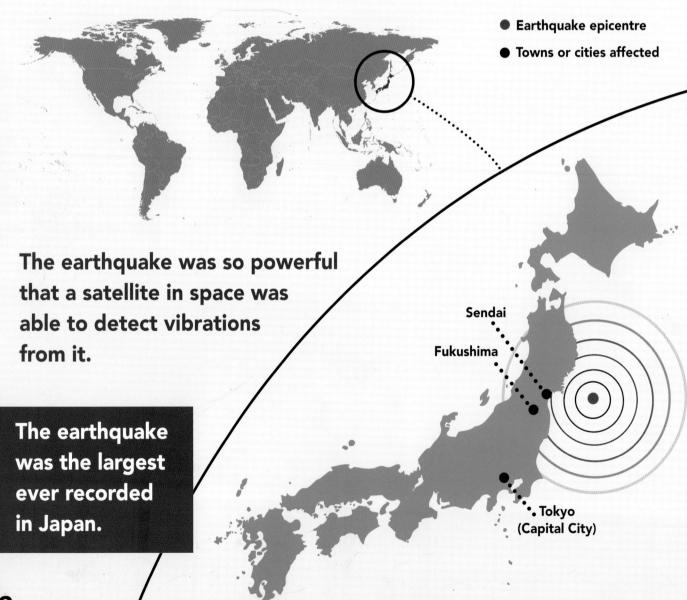

● Earthquake epicentre

● Towns or cities affected

Sendai

Fukushima

Tokyo (Capital City)

The earthquake was so powerful that a satellite in space was able to detect vibrations from it.

The earthquake was the largest ever recorded in Japan.

A tsunami, triggered by the earthquake, hit Japan and travelled up to ten kilometres inland. Almost 15,000 people died. Things got even worse when the tsunami hit the Fukushima **nuclear plant** and damaged the cooling system. A massive explosion in one of the reactors followed, which caused dangerous **radioactive** leaks. Around 300,000 people were evacuated and it is believed that the Fukushima area will not be safe to go to until at least 2021 – ten years after the radioactive leaks.

The tsunami tossed cars, homes and boats around like toys.

This little girl is wearing a mask to try to protect her from radioactive dust.

HISTORIC ERUPTIONS - VESUVIUS, TAMBORA AND KRAKATOA

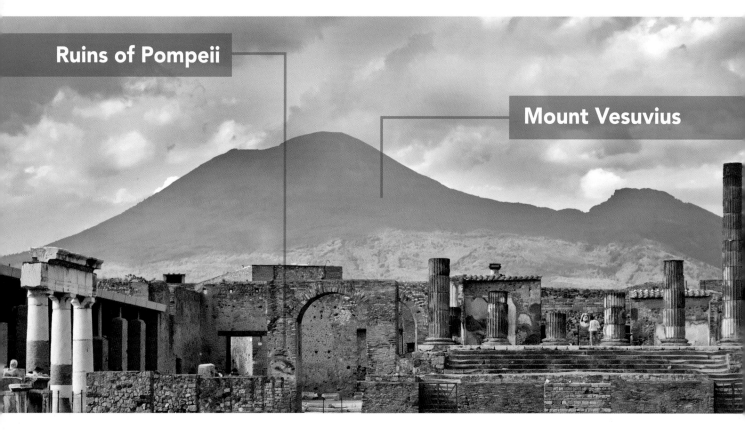

Ruins of Pompeii

Mount Vesuvius

Mount Vesuvius in Italy was thought to be an extinct volcano when it erupted in August, 79 AD. An extremely loud boom was quickly followed by hot ash raining down. A pyroclastic flow then completely buried the town of Pompeii and its inhabitants in a layer of rock, ash and cinders, seven metres deep. The nearby town of Herculaneum was also buried. Pompeii, which had been preserved by the layer of ash, was uncovered by **archaeologists** 1,700 years later.

Decayed bodies left hollows in the hardened ash. Casts of the bodies were made by filling the hollows with plaster.

A volcanic eruption blew apart the Indonesian island of Krakatoa in 1883, triggering tsunami waves 40 metres high.

In 1930, a new island appeared, formed by an undersea volcano. It is called Anak Krakatoa, meaning "Child of Krakatoa".

Anak Krakatoa erupts several times a day and is growing by 6.8 metres a year.

So much ash was thrown into the sky by the eruption of Mount Tambora in Indonesia in 1815 that the Sun was blocked out, chilling the world by 3 degrees.

The gloom caused by Tambora's eruption is thought to have inspired the spooky tale of Frankenstein, written by Mary Shelley.

MOUNT ST. HELENS AND EYJAFJALLAJOKULL

Mount St. Helens is a stratovolcano in Washington State, USA. In 1980, it was shaken by a series of earthquakes, triggering the largest landslide in history. The side of the mountain bulged like a fat tummy, before the explosive eruption that followed completely blasted away its north side, leaving a massive, jagged crater. Deadly lahars, formed from melting snow and rivers of hot ash, flattened vast areas of forest.

○ **Mount St. Helens**

The eruption changed the shape of the mountain from this ...

... to this.

Eyjafjallajokull is the name of a **glacier** that sits on top of a volcano in Iceland. In April 2010, after a series of earthquakes in the region, the volcano erupted. Spewing magma melted the glacier and released gigantic ash clouds, large enough to darken the skies over much of Europe. Ash clouds contain small, rough particles that can clog jet engines, so flights were cancelled and many people were stranded.

Ash clouds released by Eyjafjallajokull

Flights to and from Europe were cancelled.

FASCINATING FACTS

01 The word "volcano" comes from Vulcan, the Roman god of fire. He was believed to live on Mount Etna.

There are some advantages to living near a volcano. The minerals in volcanic ash help crops to grow well. Magma heats underground water, which bursts to the surface as geysers and hot springs, where people enjoy swimming. Hydrothermal (hot water) power stations use these geysers to provide cheap, renewable electricity.

02

The Old Faithful geyser in Yellowstone National Park, USA has erupted every hour for at least 100 years.

Swimmers enjoy the Blue Lagoon hot spring in Iceland.

03 A volcanic, **igneous rock** called pumice can float on water – it is the only rock that can do this. Pumice is full of holes caused by gas bubbles in the molten rock. As the rock cools and hardens, the air is trapped inside, so the rock is very light.

Pumice

04 The sound from Krakatoa reached further than any other sound in history. Over 160 kilometres away, the sound was still as loud as a jet plane taking off!

05 There is evidence that animals may be able to detect when an earthquake is coming, long before humans can. Elephants in Thailand ran to high ground hours before the 2004 tsunami happened.

VOLCANOES IN SPACE

Volcanoes exist on many of the planets and moons in our Solar System, not just on Earth. Like the Earth, these planets and moons have a mantle of molten rock, which may be forced to the surface as a volcano. Mars has many extinct volcanoes. One of these is Olympus Mons, which is the largest volcano in the Solar System. It is a shield volcano, roughly the size of Germany, and is twenty-five kilometres high. That's three times higher than Mount Everest!

Io is one of Jupiter's moons. In 1979, the Voyager 1 spacecraft recorded the first pictures of a volcano erupting in space when it passed over Io. Jupiter's volcanoes spew out sulphur dioxide.

Venus has volcanoes called pancake domes. Viewed from space, they look just like pancakes and were formed when very runny lava spread out, exactly like making pancakes in a frying pan!

GLOSSARY

archaeologists	historians who study ruins and ancient objects to learn about historical people and events
avalanches	large, often dangerous, masses of snow, ice or rock that fall away and travel at speed down a mountain
dense	tightly packed
erupts	bursts out of the ground
evacuate	to move away from an area to escape danger
geysers	hot springs that shoot out steam or hot water
glacier	a large mass of ice, moving slowly down a mountain or spreading out on a land surface
igneous rock	rock made by the action of intense heat, formed when lava cools
landslides	large amounts of earth and rock, sliding down hillsides or mountains
minerals	natural, useful and sometimes valuable substances, often obtained from the ground
molten	melted into a liquid by heat
nuclear plant	a power station that collects energy
radioactive	giving off a harmful type of energy called radiation
renewable	able to be replaced by natural processes
satellites	machines in space that travel around planets, take photographs and collect information
sulphur dioxide	a poisonous gas, released by some volcanoes
supervolcano	a giant volcanic eruption, bigger than any in recent history, which releases more than 1,000 cubic kilometres of volcanic material
tremors	shaking or trembling movements
upwind	against the direction of the wind

INDEX